ESSENTIAL STRUMS & STROKES FOR UKULELE

A TREASURY OF STRUM-HAND TECHNIQUES

Cover photo courtesy of Tom Taft Collection

To access video visit:
www.halleonard.com/mylibrary

Enter Code
1096-6356-1581-3877

ISBN 978-1-4803-3986-6

HAL•LEONARD® CORPORATION

7777 W. BLUEMOUND RD. P.O. BOX 13819 MILWAUKEE, WI 53213

In Australia Contact:
Hal Leonard Australia Pty. Ltd.
4 Lentara Court
Cheltenham, Victoria, 3192 Australia
Email: ausadmin@halleonard.com.au

Visit Hal Leonard Online at
www.halleonard.com

Contents

Introduction

It was the year 1993, while I was performing at Nash's Irish Castle in Milwaukee, when a fan walked in and gave me a beat-up, old Wendell Hall banjo uke. Not long thereafter, I became utterly fascinated with this tiny little instrument.

I discovered early on that there really wasn't much instructional material on the market to help a beginner become a proficient strummer. Even if you scoured the flea markets, antique malls, rummage sales, and music stores, you'd be more likely to find a mountain dulcimer or an accordion than anything even remotely resembling a ukulele. Nevertheless, scour I did, and eventually my search yielded a lode of old 78 records from the likes of Jimmie Rodgers, Fiddlin' Cowan Powers and his Family Band, Roy Smeck, Ukulele Ike, Johnny Marvin, Wendell Hall, George Formby, Frank Crumit, and May Singhi Breen, to name a few. Along with these ancient treasures, I also discovered many tutorials, most of which were first published in the early 20th century, including: *Wolff's Ukulele Course*, Ukulele Ike's songbooks (1, 2, and 3), the *Roy Smeck Ukulele Method*, and *Wendell Hall's Comedic Collection*, among others.

Soon I decided to make it my goal to figure out what the strum hand was capable of doing on the ukulele. I'd sit and listen to Ukulele Bailey sing "Ukulele Lady" or "Cheating On Me" (Cameo 78 #734) for hours, trying to emulate the infectious triplet strokes, slides, and rolls that I was hearing. Even Cliff Edwards (Ukulele Ike) seemed to exude an aura of tradition despite what often appeared to the ear as deceptively simple strumming.

As the years rolled on, I became the Johnny Appleseed of the ukulele, racking up 40,000 miles a year, going from one ukulele club to the next, and teaching countless classes on strum-hand techniques. Intrigued to find that these important strum-hand techniques were being under-utilized, I knew I had my work cut out for me; gladly, I accepted jobs as both a troubadour and as an educator. Looking back, I'm grateful to all of the pros who took the time to share their magic with me. I've taken their advice and have found my own way, although, I shall never forget all of these great people who nurtured my desire to become a strong strummer.

I encourage you to seek out the skills and/or work of the following educators who represent the crème de la crème of strum-hand techniques: Marcy Marxer, Joel Eckhaus, James Hill, Ralph Shaw, Peter Moss, Stu Fuchs, Ukulele Bartt, Herb Ohta, Daniel Ho, Brian Hefferan, Aaron Keim, and the late Travis Harrelson, whose inspiration lives on in this book.

May this book bode well for you, the student, combining the visual excellence of digital video with written instruction to produce a literal storehouse of strum-hand techniques that are guaranteed to provide you with a lifetime of skill-based learning! Some of these strums, like the George Formby fan stroke, have been simplified for the non-Formby fan so that the general player can easily adapt them to his or her repertoire—even if they don't already know songs like "Leaning on a Lamppost" or "When I'm Cleaning Windows."

In using this book, many of you may choose to skip around a bit, learning the strokes and strums that work best with your style. This is fine, though I would point out that pages 1–18 are meant to offer you a graduated approach to strumming. For instance, once you master the roll strokes, you will be much more successful in your attempts to master the triplets and triple rolls that are built on the heels of a flicking motion most often associated with the basic roll stroke.

Once you've mastered these exciting strokes and strums, please note that this is just the beginning! I urge you to try to attend ukulele festivals, camps, retreats, and concerts in and around your community so you can soak up the best of what the international ukulele community has to offer. All the while, keep your eyes and ears peeled for the great strummers of the world who'll be eager to pass on what they have learned to interested students like yourself.

Ukefully,
Lil' Rev
www.lilrev.com

Roy Smeck

Cliff "Ukulele Ike" Edwards

WILLIAM P. GOTTLIEB
COLLECTION (LIBRARY
OF CONGRESS)

May Singhi Breen

Wendell Hall
© BRIDGEMAN IMAGES

Roll Strokes:
The Four Essential Movements

In the early days, the lute family of instruments (think plucked instruments like mandolin, banjo, guitar, and ukulele) inspired a cadre of players who began to develop a variety of spectacular strum-hand strokes and strums. The sole purpose of these cool rhythmic techniques was to punctuate the sonic palette of a tune with a multitude of slurs, slides, tremolos, and duple-, triple-, and quadruple-meter strums. Think of a painting that is limited to just one or two colors versus one that is unencumbered by such restrictions; this is the difference between those who take the time to study classic strum-hand techniques and those who may not have had the opportunity.

Some of these strokes and strums lean heavily on the downbeat, while others employ a strong dose of syncopation via the upbeat, though more often than not, they are a fascinating combination of the two. When combined together, they make for an unstoppable strum hand. Over the years, classical, flamenco, and various western folk styles all retained a strong measure of polyrhythmic accentuation. Today, these exciting strums are still being perfected by some of the most revered practitioners of ukulele strumming.

MISSION STATEMENT

The ultimate goal of any strum-hand stroke/strum is to elevate your playing to a new level and help you make an exit out of the redundancy that is the highly repetitive down-up, down-up, down-up strum so common in ukulele circles.

One last note on roll strokes! If you're thinking that these roll strokes don't do much for you, as opposed to, say, the fan stroke or the two-finger triplet, let me be clear: *the roll stroke is the first step in learning how to do a triplet stroke.* There are no shortcuts, and the mechanics of learning to do the roll stroke will bear fruit when you move on to fancier strokes later in the book. Thus, the roll stroke is a great stand-alone strum, or it can be used to teach the flicking motion that's needed in order to execute an effective triplet stroke later on.

In the upcoming pages, we'll explore the four-finger, five-finger, three-finger, and backwards roll stroke.

James Hill

Stu Fuchs

Ralph Shaw

The Four-Finger Roll Stroke

First, I would like you to take a tiny ball of paper, set it on a table, and try to flick it off the table with your first finger. That same flicking motion is the hallmark of the roll stroke; the only difference is that we'll first start with the fourth finger, follow it with the third finger, then the second finger, and lastly the first finger.

All roll strokes are a gradual unraveling of the fingers, one at time. When done properly, the stroke makes one beat and has the sound of **r-r-r-r-r-r-r-r-r-r-r-u-p**. Think of the military band marching down the street: r-r-r-r-r-r-r-r-r-u-p–2–3–4, r-r-r-r-r-r-r-r-r-u-p–2–3–4, etc.

Let's begin:

1. Bring your fourth finger down across all four strings.

2. Follow with your third finger.

3. Now follow with your second finger.

4. Now, flick your first finger down across all four strings.

Remember, your four fingers are unraveling in a steady progression, one after the other. In the beginning, we practice one at a time slowly, but eventually, we'll speed it up until it becomes one single movement.

It helps to anchor the palm of your strum hand on the upper bout of the soundboard as you execute the four-finger roll.

Be sure to watch the video lessons throughout to get a detailed demonstration of every technique!
All of the exercises in the book are performed on the video.

Exercise

In this basic roll-stroke exercise, we are going to count "1, 2, 3, Roll," letting all four fingers unravel down across all four strings while fingering a C7 chord shape. Let's try it!

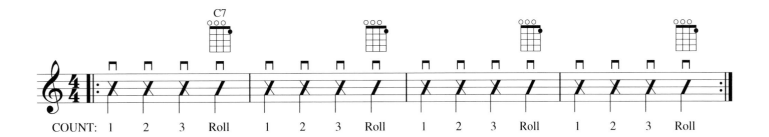

The Five-Finger Roll Stroke

Assuming that you have thoroughly practiced the four-finger roll stroke, it's time to add one more finger to the mix. Before we do, it's important to note that every roll stroke has its pros and cons. Some seem to work better in certain musical situations than others, and it's only through experimentation that you'll discover which one works best with a given tune, tempo, genre, or exercise.

The cumulative effect of all five fingers unraveling at once is a great way to add some real punch to various passages within a tune. Like the four-finger roll, it emphasizes the downbeat. Once you get good at it, this roll stroke will ring out as a single beat. However, as you learn how to do it correctly, I suggest that you start by breaking the roll into two distinct beats by first doing a four-finger roll stroke and then following it with the thumb (brushing down across all four strings). Again, the eventual goal is to roll all of the fingers and the thumb together right on the downbeat.

1. Roll all four fingers down across four strings.

2. As soon as the first finger has crossed the A string, follow immediately with the thumb, counting: 1 (four-finger roll), 2 (thumb).

Once you have mastered this initial exercise, you're ready to attempt putting these two separate movements together. Note that, unlike the four-finger roll, here you should avoid anchoring the palm of your strum hand on the ukulele. You'll want to keep your hand floating freely over the strings so the wrist can turn easily as you follow through with the thumb at the end of the stroke.

1. Start with your fingers curled in towards your palm.

2. Bring your strum-hand fourth finger down across all four strings.

3. Let your third finger follow right after your fourth finger.

4. Now your second finger follows down across all four strings.

5. Then your first finger follows down across all four strings.

6. Lastly, your thumb follows through on all four strings, completing the roll.

Exercise

For the five-finger roll stroke exercise, we'll follow the same instructions as the last, noting only that instead of using a C7 shape, we'll use A7.

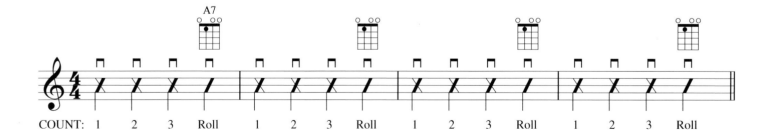

The Three-Finger Roll Stroke & Strum

After you have mastered the four- and five-finger roll stroke, it's time to look at some other ways in which you might punctuate your strumming patterns. Much like the two-finger roll stroke, which was taught in Book 1 of my instructional series, the *Hal Leonard Ukulele Method*, the three-finger roll stroke is achieved by turning the wrist rather than the typical flicking motion that happens in many of the four- and five-finger roll strokes.

What it lacks in percussion and punch, it makes up for with a sweetness that can only be described as ebullient. It looks and sounds deceptively simple but requires a strict adherence to form.

The origins of this stroke are firmly rooted in the South Sea isles of Tahiti and Fiji, where the ukulele is often approached with a uniquely Polynesian flavor. This strum-hand stroke is often held in a perpetual three-finger shape for both general strumming in a song and when employed as a roll.

As some may recall, it is most reminiscent of the "hang loose" or *shaka sign* (adopted by Hawaiian and surf culture), and once one becomes familiar with it, it is quite practical to use when you are looking to beef up and round out the quality of a song with a brighter-sounding strum.

Here's how it looks:

Alright folks! Here's how you execute this fine stroke and strum:

1. Turn the wrist in and then drag the fourth finger down across all four strings.

2. Just as the fourth finger crosses the A string, your first finger should be following immediately behind it.

3. Once the first finger has rolled past the A string, then the thumb follows gently behind to complete the three-finger movement.

Although this movement looks super simple, it really does require that you pay close attention to the detail of how you turn the wrist in and down prior to rolling all three fingers across the strings. For this, it's important that you watch the video of this movement repetitively to really get a good take on both the angle at which the wrist is cocked inwards (about 35 degrees) and the slow, deliberate manner in which you turn your wrist in a fish-hook shape. Keep in mind that you can also use this three-finger shape for a regular down-up strumming technique!

Exercise

Before we play this exercise, try to finger and review the chord sequence: C–C7–F–Fm–C–G7–C. Then position your fourth finger, first, and thumb in the hang loose shape while turning the wrist down and inwards in a fish hook pattern to create a three-finger roll. You'll strike each chord once on beat 1 of each measure.

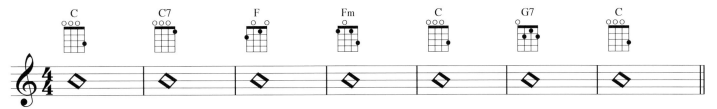

COUNT: Roll-2 - 3 - 4   Roll-2 - 3 - 4   Roll-2 - 3 - 4   Roll-2 - 3 - 4   Roll-2 - 3 - 4   Roll-2 - 3 - 4   Roll-2 - 3 - 4

The Backwards Roll Stroke

Though the backwards roll stroke is not as common as any of its derivatives, like the two- and three-finger roll strokes, it is very much a descendant of the old Madeiran people whose imprint on ukulele culture can still be felt today on the big island and beyond. The late ukulele historian John King once told me that "Madeiran publications dating back as far as 1854 could be had, which spoke of an astonishing level of proficiency on the machete (the ukulele's predecessor)."

While their repertoire of waltzes, polkas, marches, quicksteps, and mazurkas may not be as common today as they once were in the days of the late builders Manuel Nunes, Jose Do Espirito Santo, and Augusto Dias, the strum-hand techniques of these storied masters live on in the playing of today's ukulele legends like Roy Sakuma, Herb Ohta, Jake Shimabukuro, Troy Fernandez, Dr. Byron Yasui, and Kimo Hussey.

As we learn how to play a backwards roll, in time you may discover that employing this stroke is not unlike that of many other vaudeville or novelty strokes—such as the zig-zag or figure eight—in that it is both highly percussive and visually appealing all at once. What's unique about it is also what makes it funky: it starts with an upstroke!

Here's how the starting position looks:

1. To begin, make a C chord with your fret hand and place your strum hand at 45 degree angle above the strings while resting your thumb on the edge of the fretboard (10th fret).

2. Bring the pad of your fourth finger up across all four strings.

3. Just as the fourth finger crosses the G string, you'll follow the fourth finger with the pad of the third finger up across all four strings.

4. As the third finger crosses the G string, follow in an upwards motion with the pad of the second finger up across all four strings.

5. Lastly, as the second finger crosses the G string, follow it with the pad of the first finger to complete the stroke.

Exercise

Before playing the following exercise, take a moment to finger each chord form. Please note that the C#°7 in measure 4 may be new to many of you. Next practice counting "Roll, 2, 3–and, 4," and say it to yourself a couple of times. *Note:* The backwards roll stroke starts with an upstroke, which is unlike all of the other roll strokes and thus may take some getting used to.

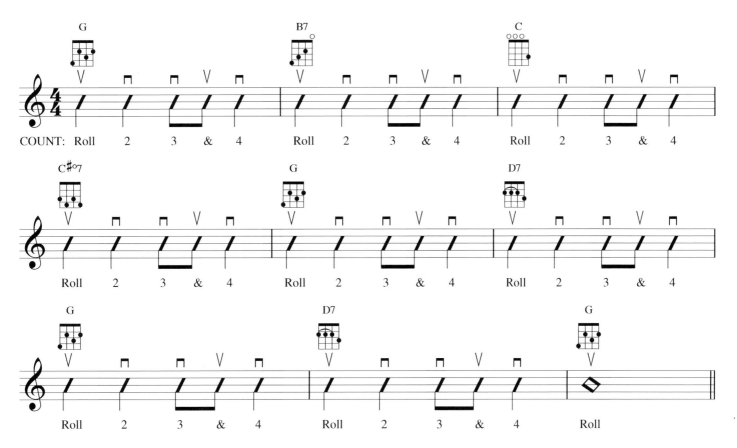

PHOTO COURTESY OF THE LIL' REV ARCHIVE

Hanging out with the late John King at the 2008 New York Uke Festival. John was a huge influence on so many of us. He was not only one of the most virtuosic campanella and fingerstyle players around, John was a walking encyclopedia of ukulele history and lore.

Practical Approaches to Playing Tremolo

Tremolo can be defined as a rapid reiteration of a musical tone when a series of notes are played quickly without worrying too much about the exact number played. I often tell my students to think of a sound meter and the little needle that displays as low, mid, high, or redline. When the sound is too loud, the little needle is in the red; when it's too soft, it can hardly be seen. When practicing tremolo on the ukulele, try to keep that imaginary needle vibrating straight up at 12 o'clock, and learn to keep it there with just the right amount of force applied to the strings in continuous alternating strokes. As you begin, start slowly with a down-up motion and then gradually build up speed until there is a continuous, smooth, flowing sound.

Before I begin to teach you a variety of ways in which you can play tremolo on the ukulele, let me highlight some songs for which the technique would be well-suited: "In the Still of the Night," "Stand by Me," "Tennessee Waltz," "Goodnight Irene," "Those Were the Days My Friend," "Yesterday," "Crazy," "Teenager in Love," "Michelle," "Sea of Love," and "Blue Moon," to name a few.

Claw-Shaped Tremolo

The first approach we'll study is referred to as a *claw-shaped tremolo.* Here's how it looks:

Here's how it's done:

Point all of the fingers on your strum hand straight out and then curl your first finger down so that when holding the ukulele, as if to strum, you have just one finger that'll be touching the strings.

Exercise

For this exercise, we'll practice using the claw-shaped tremolo over a standard doo-wop progression of G–Em–C–D7. Keep your tremolo moving in a rapid down-up motion.

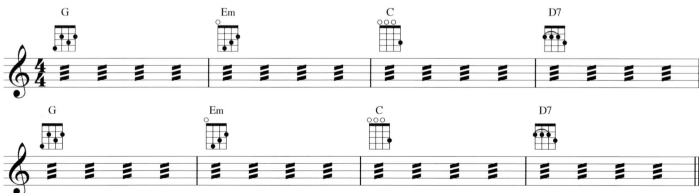

Note: As you practice the claw-shaped tremolo, keep the first finger focused on the two middle strings (C and E). Then gradually move the finger down and up enough to encompass all four strings, just as you begin to get it going at a steady rate.

Pick-Style Tremolo

While there are many options for playing tremolo, few of them offer as much control as the approach I am about to teach you. The *pick-style* approach supports the first finger by resting the thumb on it for stabilization. Many players find this to be much less of a challenge than letting one single finger (as in the claw-shaped motion) do all the work. Thus, the thumb supports the first finger and helps maintain solid control without the sort of fatigue that happens when a single finger is used exclusively.

For example, if you have ever held a guitar pick or plectrum of any sort in your hand, then you may find this to be a natural fit. Here's how it looks:

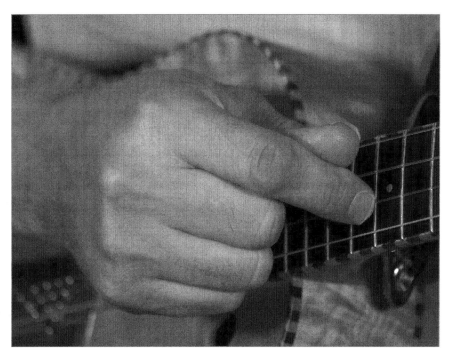

And here's how it's done:

1. Start by making the squirt gun shape with your strum hand.

2. Bring your thumb to rest on your first finger about one inch down from the tip of the finger (at first crease).

3. Rest it gently—just enough for the finger to feel supported by the thumb.

4. The other fingers can either hang down, or you can tuck them in by making a partial fist.

Exercise

Let's try this on for size and see how it feels with a warm-up exercise. To begin, let's play this jug-band blues progression from the late '20s using a slow tempo. This will allow you to really hear the benefits of using a pick-style tremolo.

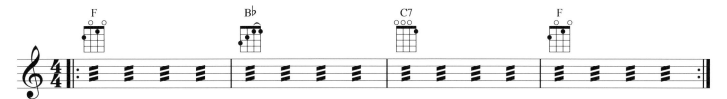

The Ending Tremolo Technique

Chances are you've heard the ending tremolo technique a million times but never knew what it was called. It's used so often, across a wide continuum of stringed instruments, that people have come to expect it at live concerts of pop, rock, and country, to blues and even bluegrass music! It works like a charm on the ukulele, and I consider it to be like frosting on the cake insofar as it always adds a nice sweet, finishing touch to the end of a song.

Here's how you do it:

1. Place your thumb in the juncture at the base, where the neck meets the body of the ukulele.

2. Point your middle finger down towards the strings, while the others hang straight out.

3. Next, bring the fleshy pad of your middle finger up across all four strings starting with the A. This movement should be fast and steady.

4. Now, using the skills you learned mastering the four-finger roll stroke, flick your middle finger back down.

Once you get good at this down-up, down-up, down-up movement, it should begin to take on the quality of a steady pulse.

Note: Remember, the down-up movement is highly repetitive and will initially require a little bit of practice to get the muscles and tendons of the middle finger flexible enough to maintain a sustained pulse. Don't be discouraged if it feels awkward or clumsy at first; it will become more consistent with every attempt.

Exercise

First familiarize yourself with each chord shape and strike each twice, counting "1, 2, 3, 4." Then finger the last F chord and apply the ending tremolo technique.

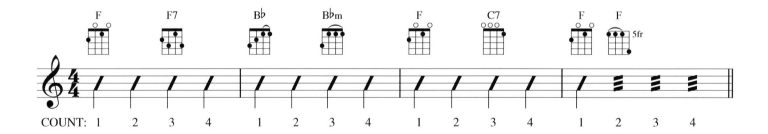

The Zig-Zag Stroke

The *zig-zag stroke* is a legendary vaudeville-era stroke. Early purveyors like Roy Smeck, Frank Crumit, Johnny Marvin, and May Singhi Breen sought to capitalize on both its visual appeal as well as its highly rhythmic effect, when alternated with a common down-up strum.

The secret to this stroke is to use it sparingly over the course of a song. For instance, perhaps you'd strum a basic down-up strum over the verses and then add the zig-zag over the chorus or refrain. Remember, the zig-zag stroke adds both visual appeal as well as a unique variation to whatever rhythm your song calls for at its onset.

- You may use short, tight strokes or long loose strokes up and down the fretboard.
- There aren't any rules as to which fingers to use when applying the zig-zag stroke.
- The only rule of thumb is to keep the zig-zag going in a down-up pattern. That's it!

Here's how to do it:

1. Position the ukulele so the body is resting on your right leg with your fret hand gently holding the neck up. You'll want to free yourself from having to brace the ukulele against your body, but rather rest it on your knee or use a strap so your right arm is free to move about unencumbered once you apply the zig-zag motion. (Left-handed folks should reverse these directions.)

2. To practice the motion, first take any combination of strum-hand fingers and draw an imaginary line down and up the fretboard without touching the strings. This will prepare you for actually doing the zig-zag stroke.

   - Work your way down the fretboard as well as back up (reversing the same strum pattern).
   - The only rule is to keep the fingers moving in a zig-zag pattern (down-up).
   - You may double up on the downstroke at the start of each line, up or down the neck.

3. Now, take your fret hand and dampen the strings (no need to fret a chord or note). Then run the finger(s) of your strum hand down and up the fretboard in a zig-zag pattern, creating a muted sound.

4. The last step is to find a simple two- or three-chord song to practice this stroke. Some of my favorite pieces would include "Four Reasons," "Ain't No Bugs on Me," "Ain't She Sweet," "Five Foot Two," "Ukulele Lady," "Dinah," and "Mr. Crump."

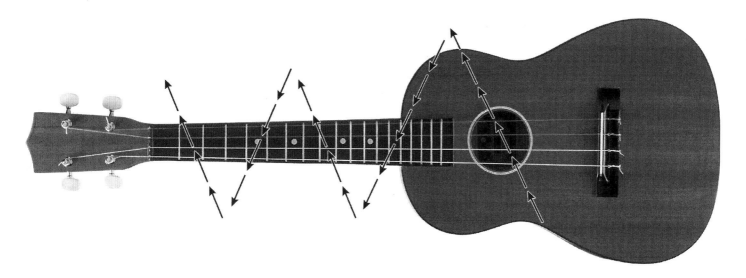

Learning to Play
Triplets on the Ukulele

When it comes to strumming the ukulele, one thing is for certain: the *triplet stroke* is the pinnacle of great strum-hand technique. The sound is at once distinctive and addictive to the ear. While this stroke may not always come easy due to its syncopated feel, it's always been the single most rewarding strum to master on the ukulele.

Before we learn how to execute a triplet stroke, let's take a moment to talk about what a triplet is in musical terms. A *triplet* is a group of notes played inside another note length; in other words, it's a portion of musical time that is split rhythmically into three equal parts. Thus, a triplet can be identified by a small "3" above or below its note beam or bracket. A triplet group's total duration is equal to two of the original note values contained within.

Examples might include an eighth-note triplet, which spans the length of two eighth notes (one quarter note), or a quarter-note triplet, which spans the length of a half note, and so on.

For example:

Note that, in a 4/4 song when a few triplet strokes might be added, the time signature doesn't change; it remains in 4/4. You'll find that the triplets are always marked with a little number "3" as mentioned earlier. Remember that this means *three notes are played in the space usually taken by two.* Thus, the three beamed notes take one beat or one foot tap to the floor.

Here are some other important notes about performing the triplet stroke:

- The emphasis is on the first beat; count "**1–2–3, 1–2–3,** etc."

- Many students find it helpful to say, "Trip-a-let" or "Hard-soft-soft."

- This bears repeating: the emphasis is always on the first beat.

The Two-Finger-and-Thumb Triplet

The *two-finger-and-thumb triplet* is a variation on the first-finger-and-thumb triplet, so you can play it either way and it will still be effective. I have found over the years that my students have better control with the flicking motion that this stroke requires when using two fingers versus just one.

Here's how the starting position looks:

Now let's try it:

1. Flick your first two fingers together down across all four strings.

2. Follow this with your thumb, brushing down across all four strings.

3. Finally, come up with your first two fingers together to complete the stroke and then start all over again. Repeat until this pattern becomes a continuous motion.

Many of my regular students have found it very helpful to think of the "little train that could" analogy. In other words, start off the pattern very slowly at first and then gradually build up enough speed to keep the stroke flowing consistently in a down-down-up manner. It may take weeks or months to condition the muscles and tendons of your hand to accomplish this, but don't give up! Create a regular practice routine of three minutes at a time, three to four times a week, and you will definitely start to see results.

Exercise

Using three very simple open-position chords, count "**1–2–3, 1–2–3**" for each triplet. This exercise will not only help you master the two-finger-and-thumb triplet, but it will simultaneously help you practice using a triplet stroke while changing chords.

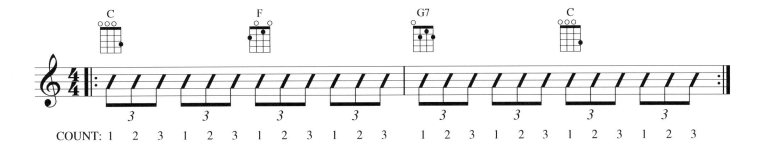

Lil' Rev's Two-Finger Triplet

Technically, a triplet can be executed with any combination of fingers. In my travels around the globe, I have seen more variations on this theme than any other strum-hand stroke. The *two-finger triplet* is unique in that it is one of the only triplet forms that does not employ the use of the thumb as part of its **1–2–3** pattern.

Over the years, this stroke has become my signature triplet and is also a real winner when it comes to clarity of tone, speed, and ease of control. The simple fact of the matter is that triplets that involve the thumb can often sound disjointed when compared to the two-finger approach.

There are three movements to this triplet, which will follow a down-up-up pattern. Let's begin:

1. To begin, make a fist and rest the fleshy part of the thumb near the upper bout of the ukulele.

2. Then flick your first and second fingers together down across all four strings.

3. Third, come up across all four strings with your first finger.

4. To complete the pattern, finish by bringing the second finger up across all four strings. Continue to repeat this pattern over and over, first slowly, and then gradually building momentum until you can maintain a good speed.

Exercise

Try practicing the two-finger triplet using an A–D–E7–A progression.

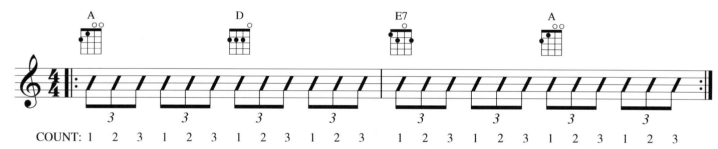

Lil' Rev

The Travis Harrelson Triple Roll

During the twilight years of vaudeville (1915–1925), many enterprising and studious strummers began to experiment with combining roll strokes and triplets into a single strum. Today, we commonly call this a *triple roll*. Travis Harrelson of Seal Beach, California, was one of the many important links in that chain and is the reason why I, too, am passing this along to you.

Travis passed away at 80 years of age in August of 2010. He was a consummate player, jazz aficionado, and someone who'd been strumming since his childhood in the '30s. Unfortunately, this great master did not leave behind a huge body of recorded work nor videos for us to study. You can see and hear him on Jumping Jim's *Joys of Uke* DVD, the documentary *Rock That Uke*, and on his 2008 CD release called *Holy Ukuleles* with Eddie Montana.

Travis was a perfect gentleman who welcomed many of us into his home and loved to jam the old standards with anyone who was willing. I am still amazed at what Travis was able to do with his strum hand. It was a thing of beauty and grace. To this day, no one really knows how to explain how he did it!

What Travis learned from others, he always made his own, so I adapted his remarkable triple-roll strum to the best of my ability and now I pass it on to you.

The many faces of Travis Harrelson

Here's how to do it:

1. Start by counting "**1**–2–3–**1**, **1**–2–3–**1**, **1**–2–3–**1**, **1**–2–3–**1**." Note that the emphasis is on the first "1" and the second "1."

2. Then go back to pages 7 and 8 to review the four- and five-finger roll strokes.

3. Rest the fleshy part of the thumb on the upper bout of the ukulele with your fingers curled up in a fist.

4. Next, unravel all four fingers down across all four strings just like you would do for a four-finger roll.

5. Just as soon as the first finger crosses the A string on its way down, the thumb follows right behind it, also in a downward motion.

6. Once the thumb has also crossed the A string, follow by coming up with your first and second fingers in concert with one another.

7. To complete the stroke, flick your first and second fingers down across all four strings.

Exercise

To practice the Harrelson triple roll, we'll use a classic ragtime ending! Count "**1**–2–3–**1**" (down–down–up–down) for each chord.

George Formby

George Hoy Booth, commonly known as George Formby, was born in Lancashire, England, in May of 1904. George's father (who also went by the name George Formby) was an entertainer and comedian par excellence who seemed to have passed the torch onto his son at the time of his unexpected death in 1921. George came of age in the early '20s as vaudeville and Broadway were casting a bright light across North America and the whole of England's Music Hall tradition.

Fascinated with the ukulele, and in particular Wendell Hall and Cliff "Ukulele Ike" Edwards, George accepted a bet that "he dare not use the banjo-ukulele in his act." He proceeded to bring down the house at his Alhambra Theatre gig in Bransley.

Today, his legacy is joyfully carried on by a legion of virtuosic Formby aficionados, including Andy Eastwood, Peter Moss, and Ralph Shaw, to name a few. The largest legion of Formby fans stay connected via the George Formby Society (http://www.georgeformby.co.uk/), which organizes quarterly conventions throughout the year to celebrate all things Formby and attracts some of the world's greatest players.

A Look at His Style

A close-up look at George Formby's strum-hand techniques reveals a "less is more" school of percussive strumming, which he relied on to great effect. His songs showcase a bulldozer-like common-stroke (down-up) combined with thumb-drags, triplets, triple rolls, fan strokes, hammer-ons, pull-offs, chord slurs, and split strokes. Due to the fascinating way in which George combined all of these strum-hand strokes and strums, he managed to produce one of the most imitated bodies of work across a continuum peppered with the likes of Roy Smeck, Cliff Edwards, Johnny Marvin, Wendell Hall, and countless others. What is even more amazing is how he managed to create a style that was all his own while also sounding so timeless and authentic given the nature of his repertoire, which was rooted in double-entendre and comedic verse.

George favored the banjo-uke.
© PICTORIAL PRESS LTD / ALAMY

George was immensely popular amongst WWII soldiers.
© RONALD GRANT ARCHIVE / ALAMY

The Simplified Fan Stroke

The simplified fan stroke is a fool-proof stroke that should be used sparingly to create rhythmic nuance—either during a chord-based solo or intermittently throughout a given progression. The following approach is a simplified version of the full-blown fan stroke that I have arranged for the non-Formby strummer. This is done with the hopes that you will soon add these exciting strums to your own repertoire, be it blues, jazz, old-time, bluegrass, country, rock, pop, or punk. Once you have mastered this stroke, I hope you will take some time to listen to George Formby recordings and seek out his numerous film clips to deepen your study of his style.

Here's how to do it:

1. Begin by dampening the strings with the fret hand.

2. Make a fist with the strum hand and rest the fleshy part of the thumb against the upper left-front of the body, just as you would if you were going to do a roll stroke.

3. Flick the fourth finger down and diagonally out across all four strings (repetition is the key to gaining the control needed to execute this movement).

4. Follow the fourth finger with the thumb, brushing it straight down across all four strings.

5. Lastly, bring the first finger up diagonally towards the upper right bout of the ukulele.

Note: Count "**1**–2–3," with the hand opening on "**1**" and closing right after the first finger comes up on "3." This will create the visual effect of a fan as the hand opens and closes repetitively. Start slowly at first and then gradually try to build up speed. Think of the "little train that could" analogy and strive to control this stroke at both slow and fast tempos.

Exercise
Count "**1**–2–3, **1**–2–3" all the way through until the last measure, which ends on one single fourth-finger downstroke.

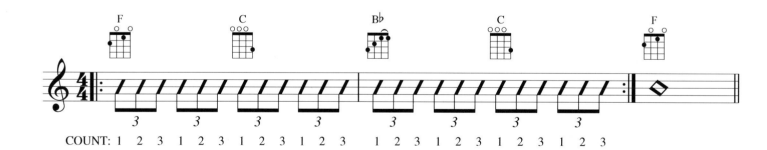

The Palm Muting Technique

Palm muting is a strum-hand technique that applies to many different styles of playing, including blues, jazz, rock, R&B, country, and more. It's an important technique for creating some rhythmic variation within a song and also offers you a chance to manipulate the melody line of a tune with an exciting "thump-like" effect.

Chances are, if you grew up listening to country twang, rock, pop, metal, or grunge, you've already heard this sound a million times on the guitar and need only a little instruction to appreciate how effective it can be in your arsenal of strum-hand tricks. To do this, I'm going to teach you how to use palm muting with some rock 'n' roll power chords and a simple bluegrass melody. I think you'll find this to be a fun technique that you can employ from time to time, though the uninitiated ukulele fan will be pleasantly surprised to hear you doing this on a uke (versus the guitar or bass where it's most at home).

To begin:

1. Lightly rest the heel, or palm, of your strum hand on the strings just above (or before) the bridge.

    • If you rest your palm too lightly, the strings will ring out just like they would if they were being played open.

    • If you apply too much force, you'll dampen the strings to the point where there won't be any tone at all.

2. Now take your fret hand and fret a C5 power chord (this could technically be any chord). It looks like this:

3. Once you have the C5 chord fretted, gently rest the palm of your strum hand on the strings above the bridge and then begin brushing down across the C, E, and A strings with your thumb. You should hear the slightly muffled sound of a C5 chord ring out. Let's do this a few times.

Note: This takes some getting used to, but once you have a bit of practice, you can employ this technique with either chords or melody.

Exercise

Count "1–and–2–and–3–and–4–and" for each measure. Remember to keep your palm's heel resting lightly on all three strings in order to get that muted sound.

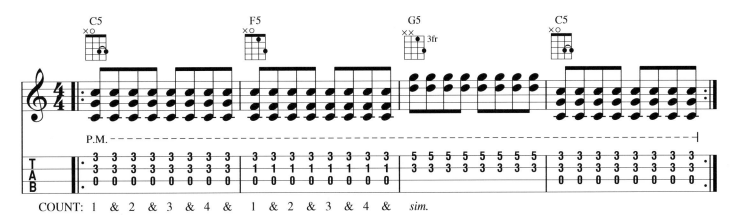

Palm Muting with a Basic Bluegrass Melody

Now that we've had a little practice using the palm muting technique over multiple strings, one note at a time should be fairly easy. Before we attempt to use palm muting with a simple melody, let's familiarize ourselves with the basic melodic structure of the tune "Boil 'Em Cabbage Down."

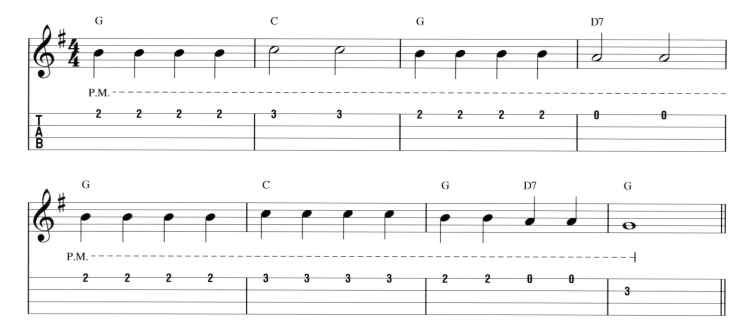

Now we'll use the same approach that we used when palm muting chords to palm mute the individual notes of "Boil 'Em Cabbage Down."

To review:

1. Rest the palm of your strum hand gently over the strings just above the bridge.

2. Use the palm to mute the E and A strings while the thumb picks the muted melody.

3. Return to the melody above and try it once again, but this time apply the palm muting technique (P.M.).

Ukulele Bartt Wharburton

is a California-based ukulele master

who combines rock, metal, flamenco,

and classical influences to produce

a delightful fusion of fretboard

pyrotechnics and musical

mayhem wherever he goes.

The Simplified Doo-Wop Strum

For as long as I can remember, America has had a never-ending fascination with the doo-wop era. They were tunes just as easily sung on the street corner as on a concert stage, and they left an indelible mark on American popular music that isn't likely to go away anytime soon. The music was popularized by groups like the Del Vikings ("Come Go with Me"), the Tokens ("The Lion Sleeps Tonight"), the Chimes ("I'm in the Mood for Love"), the Marcels ("Blue Moon"), and 1957's million-selling hit by the Silhouettes titled "Get a Job."

Doo-wop added fuel to the rock 'n' roll fire while leaning heavily on R&B and soul. It was the catalyst for countless Beatles songs and added a wholesome counterpart to the oft-misunderstood generations of the '50s and '60s. They were clean-cut, well-dressed, and drenched in luscious vocal harmonies sweet enough to win the affection of mom and daughter alike; after all, who could argue with the Chords as they sang "Sh-Boom, Sh-Boom" or the Shirelles' "Will You Love Me Tomorrow?" Ukulele clubs the world over have embraced this repertoire and for good reason: it's fun, easy to play, sounds great, and everyone seems to know this body of work well enough to sing along.

Here's what the typical doo-wop chord progression sounds like in a few keys. Try strumming these progressions a few times in 6/8 time while counting "1–2–3, 1–2–3" over each chord change. Soon you'll hear the reason why this chord progression has been given its own name by musicians near and far.

1. **Key of B♭**: B♭–Gm–E♭–F7

2. **Key of C**: C–Am–F–G7

3. **Key of F**: F–Dm–B♭–C7

4. **Key of G**: G–Em–C–D

5. **Key of A**: A–F♯m–D–E7

Exercise

Using your thumb to brush down across all four strings, let's use Example #2 from above (key of C), counting "1–2–3, **1**–2–3," over each chord change, putting the accent on the second "1."

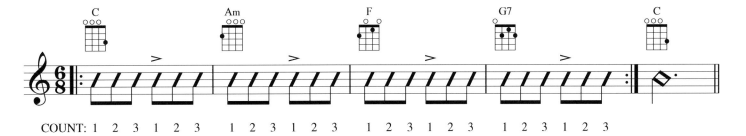

Once you've mastered this fabulous strum using the thumb, consider trying it with the two-finger triplet or the fan stroke. See the video for demonstrations of each.

This chord progression sounds great any way you slice it, so why not experiment with tremolo, roll strokes, or any other cool strum-hand techniques you have learned in this book.

The Whammy Technique

Anyone who's ever strummed an acoustic uke knows all too well that it has almost no sustain. Strummed chords and picked melody notes tend to fade faster than you can say "my dog has fleas!" For those players who might have come to the ukulele via the electric guitar or bass, they'll surely be nostalgic for more sustain. The *whammy technique* is a cool way to simulate what one might do if the ukulele had a whammy bar.

How it works:

1. Rest the base or your strum hand slightly behind the bridge.

2. Using your thumb, pluck the open C string and then immediately fan your hand up and down toward the strings of the ukulele without actually touching them. The motion comes from pivoting the hand from the wrist.

Once mastered, this technique can be used for both melodic playing as well as chord work. It sounds great with surf, Hawaiian, rock, blues, and even jazz styles. Here are a few exercises designed to help you master this super cool strum-hand technique!

Exercises

To begin, use your thumb to practice playing the notes of the C major scale in first position.

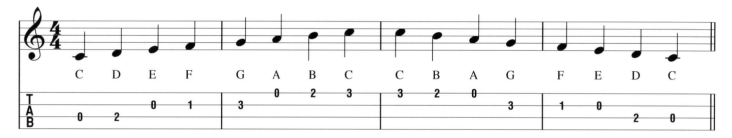

Once you're familiar with the C major scale and can pick it confidently, try it again a few more times using the whammy technique, fanning each individual note.

Jake Shimabukuro

is truly a remarkable

player in every way.

Watch his strum hand;

it's a thing of beauty!

The next exercise uses the whammy technique with chords instead of individual melody notes like the previous exercise. This classic jazz-era intro is known as the "Blackbird intro." Take a moment to familiarize yourself with these chord shapes.

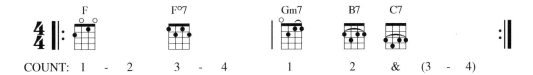

To begin, return to the chord progression above and brush each chord once with the thumb followed by the whammy technique. The Gm7 and B7 chords are the only ones that are struck just once without the use of the whammy technique. Instead, you'll strike each chord for one beat and then go directly to the C7 on the "and" of beat 2, which you'll strike and then follow with the whammy technique.

Again, the sequence will be as follows:

1. Strike the F chord and then apply the whammy technique.

2. Next, strike the F°7 chord and apply the whammy technique.

3. Third, strike the Gm7.

4. Strike the B7 once and then, rather quickly, brush the C7 with added whammy technique to end.

Marcy Marxer is not only one of the sweetest folks in the ukulele world, but also one of the most versatile players I have ever met. She moves seamlessly between jazz, blues, swing, old time, rockabilly, folk, world, and her own songs! She's a former student of the late Roy Smeck and can really throw down some mean strum-hand strokes!

The Old-Time Waltz Strum

The *old-time waltz strum* is also known as the three-quarter-time stroke, which means that there are three quarter notes per measure. This time signature is symbolized by a large number three resting over the number four ($\frac{3}{4}$).

In the old days, this was referred to as "**OOM**–pah–pah, **OOM**–pah–pah," and most folks were familiar with the old fashioned slow dance known as the *waltz*. For those of you who read music, remember the following with regard to 3/4 time:

$$\quarternote + \quarternote + \quarternote = \dottedhalfnote$$

$$\dottedhalfnote = \halfnote + \quarternote$$

$$\halfnote + \quarternote = \quarternote + \halfnote$$

Some of the greatest songs in 3/4 time are "Home on the Range," "Nights in White Satin," "America," "Wonderful World," "Little Boxes," "Silent Night," "Amazing Grace," "Norwegian Wood," "Mr. Bojangles," "Tennessee Waltz," and "So Long, It's Been Good to Know Yuh," to name but a few.

Eventually you'll find yourself at a local song circle, jam, or open mic, and when you do, be ready! It won't be long before someone begins to sing a song in 3/4 time.

Here's how it works:

1. Make a C chord with your fret hand.
2. Strum down with your first finger or thumb and count "1."
3. Strum down again and follow with a quick upstroke, counting "2–and."
4. Lastly, strum down one last time to end while counting "3."

The whole thing looks like this:

COUNT: 1   2 & 3

Exercise

Now let's practice this strum with a basic F–B♭–C7 chord progression.

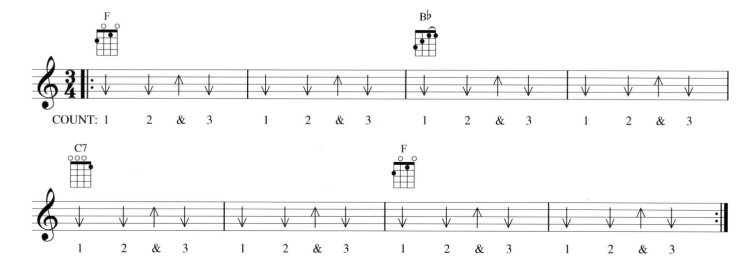

The Clawhammer Stroke

Originally, this highly syncopated banjo stroke was the sole domain of Afro-American songsters of the American south. Soon, their influence found its way into the hands of their Anglo contemporaries and began to spread far and wide via the minstrel and medicine show circuit. Today, the early styles of playing are still being emulated and perfected by a whole new generation of young pickers, eager to carry on the authentic folkways of America.

The reentrant tuning (G–C–E–A and A–D–F♯–B) of the ukulele lends itself well to playing with a clawhammer approach, since the high G acts like the fifth string on a banjo, which is used as a drone string. The stroke itself works well when used as accompaniment for the voice or as a vehicle for playing melody.

For well over 100 years, this banjo stroke was primarily passed on through oral traditions. To really get this down, you'll need to watch the video multiple times. The syncopation of this stroke bears repeating, so stay with it and you'll be playing "Old Joe Clark" in no time! When this stroke is performed accurately, it makes a "bum-dit-ty" sound. Once you can play the basic stroke, then you'll be ready to integrate it into song accompaniment or melody.

Let's see how it works:

1. With your fret hand, make a G chord.

2. With your strum hand, curl the fingers of your hand into a claw-like shape and cock the thumb so that it angles down 15 degrees or so.

3. Using the nail of your first finger, strike the D note (C string, 2nd fret). This is the "bum."

4. Next, brush down across the entire G chord with that same finger. This is the "dit."

5. As your nail brushes down across the G chord, your thumb should come to rest on the high G string. (That's right! You need a high G to make this really work.) As it does, bear down on it with just enough pressure to push the string down and out ever so slightly, thereby creating a popping sound which we'll refer to as the "ty."

Exercise
Try the technique out with this little example.

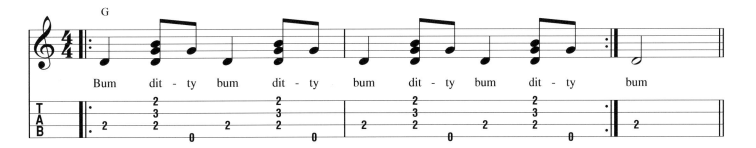

Once you've mastered this slowly, gradually build up speed and then try to tackle some basic fiddle tunes like "Boil 'Em Cabbage Down," "Buffalo Gals," "Cripple Creek," and "Red Wing." You might also consider trying to find a local banjo instructor in your town who can help you refine this movement and thereby integrate some more advanced approaches. While most may be content to strum the ukulele, the clawhammer stroke opens up a world of possibilities for playing roots-based music and is well worth the extra effort it takes to master.

The Punk Rock Strum

Ukulele players are notorious for relying on the common stroke—i.e., simple down-up, down-up strumming. As a result, I've found it beneficial to teach the *punk rock strum* to almost everyone in an effort to establish a strong sense of playing on the downbeat. You needn't dress in leather, spike your hair, nor limit yourself to just three chords to appreciate the value of punk rock, but it wouldn't hurt you to give a listen to some of the genre's real legends like the Sex Pistols, the Ramones, Television, the Damned, the Clash, the Dead Boys, the Stooges, the New York Dolls, or the Violent Femmes (on the folk punk side).

Remember, even if punk isn't your thing, the real point of this lesson is to help you develop a strong, consistent downstroke. Once you are comfortable with this strum, you'll be able to apply it to rock, blues, pop, country, grunge, punk, and metal.

Here's how it works:

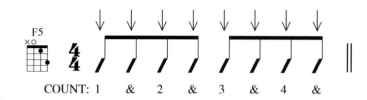

1. To begin, finger an F5 chord.

2. Then use your thumb, pick, or first finger to brush down on the chord, playing hard and fast while counting "1–and–2–and–3–and–4–and."

Remember to use all downstrokes. While I play with my thumb and fingers 99% of the time, occasionally when playing fast rock 'n' roll, I like to use a guitar pick or felt ukulele pick to give me a little more of an edge.

Exercise

Ok, now let's mix it up a bit! This time we'll be using F5, Bb5, and C5. Remember to count "1–and–2–and–3–and–4–and" in each 4/4 measure.

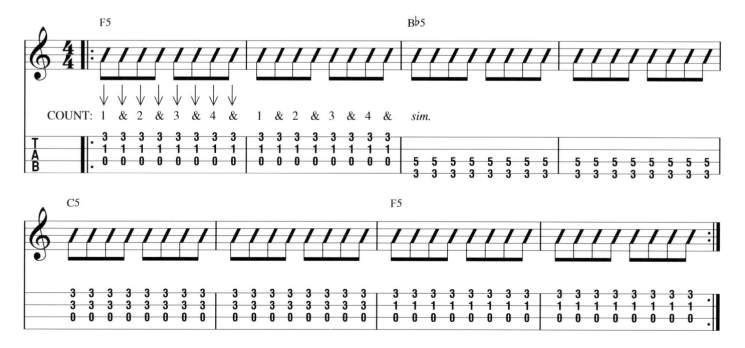

Here are some favored punk- and rock-based chord forms that would be helpful to know:

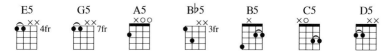

Chord Chart

MAJOR	MINOR	7TH	POWER
C	Cm	C7	C5
D	Dm	D7	D5
E	Em	E7	E5
F	Fm	F7	F5
G	Gm	G7	G5
A	Am	A7	A5
B♭	B♭m	B♭7	B♭5
B	Bm	B7	B5

Hal•Leonard®
UKULELE
PLAY-ALONG

1. POP HITS
00701451 Book/CD Pack $15.99

3. HAWAIIAN FAVORITES
00701453 Book/Online Audio $14.99

4. CHILDREN'S SONGS
00701454 Book/Online Audio $14.99

5. CHRISTMAS SONGS
00701696 Book/CD Pack $12.99

6. LENNON & MCCARTNEY
00701723 Book/Online Audio $12.99

7. DISNEY FAVORITES
00701724 Book/Online Audio $14.99

8. CHART HITS
00701745 Book/CD Pack $15.99

9. THE SOUND OF MUSIC
00701784 Book/CD Pack $14.99

10. MOTOWN
00701964 Book/CD Pack $12.99

11. CHRISTMAS STRUMMING
00702458 Book/Online Audio $12.99

12. BLUEGRASS FAVORITES
00702584 Book/CD Pack $12.99

13. UKULELE SONGS
00702599 Book/CD Pack $12.99

14. JOHNNY CASH
00702615 Book/Online Audio $15.99

15. COUNTRY CLASSICS
00702834 Book/CD Pack $12.99

16. STANDARDS
00702835 Book/CD Pack $12.99

17. POP STANDARDS
00702836 Book/CD Pack $12.99

18. IRISH SONGS
00703086 Book/Online Audio $12.99

19. BLUES STANDARDS
00703087 Book/CD Pack $12.99

20. FOLK POP ROCK
00703088 Book/CD Pack $12.99

21. HAWAIIAN CLASSICS
00703097 Book/CD Pack $12.99

22. ISLAND SONGS
00703098 Book/CD Pack $12.99

23. TAYLOR SWIFT
00221966 Book/Online Audio $16.99

24. WINTER WONDERLAND
00101871 Book/CD Pack $12.99

25. GREEN DAY
00110398 Book/CD Pack $14.99

26. BOB MARLEY
00110399 Book/Online Audio $14.99

27. TIN PAN ALLEY
00116358 Book/CD Pack $12.99

28. STEVIE WONDER
00116736 Book/CD Pack $14.99

29. OVER THE RAINBOW & OTHER FAVORITES
00117076 Book/Online Audio $15.99

30. ACOUSTIC SONGS
00122336 Book/CD Pack $14.99

31. JASON MRAZ
00124166 Book/CD Pack $14.99

32. TOP DOWNLOADS
00127507 Book/CD Pack $14.99

33. CLASSICAL THEMES
00127892 Book/Online Audio $14.99

34. CHRISTMAS HITS
00128602 Book/CD Pack $14.99

35. SONGS FOR BEGINNERS
00129009 Book/Online Audio $14.99

36. ELVIS PRESLEY HAWAII
00138199 Book/Online Audio $14.99

37. LATIN
00141191 Book/Online Audio $14.99

38. JAZZ
00141192 Book/Online Audio $14.99

39. GYPSY JAZZ
00146559 Book/Online Audio $15.99

40. TODAY'S HITS
00160845 Book/Online Audio $14.99

HAL•LEONARD®
www.halleonard.com

Prices, contents, and availability subject to change without notice.